Site of Disappearance

Erin Malone

ORNITHOPTER PRESS   PRINCETON

First Edition

Published by Ornithopter Press
www.ornithopterpress.com

ISBN 978-1-942723-16-5

Library of Congress Control Number: 2023942155

Cover image:
The Visitor, oil and graphite on panel, 2009
by Ryan Molenkamp
www.ryanmolenkamp.com
courtesy of the artist

Design and composition by Mark Harris

Contents

I.

II.

III.

IV.

V.

~

The way to keep something is to forget it.
Then it goes to an enormous place.

—Jenny George

Site of Disappearance

I.

Biography

my brother was born blue / and quiet / not unlike the sky and like the sky he lived / exposed / blueberry mouth blue eyes his heart / tied in a bow / the river threading his wrist / a slow river lazy / boat his heartbeat / his echo / lived / his name scribbled / in my books / his hop-step laugh on the loop / of our neighborhood trailed me / bugged me / his leg brace / his bracelet warning / labels / his sirens his strokes / he lived / his freckled skin his / surgeons his open / heart / his staples his scars / his tracks / this sky / he lived / for eleven years he lived / and then /

Swing the Statue

Fireflies strung, the lilac evening
beaded on the drinks in our fathers'

raised hands. Our fathers didn't turn
from the patios; our mothers practiced

eternity. In this game only I could move.
Time stands still because

it has a body—My brothers and
the kids from our cul-de-sac

fell where I flung them, landed as tigers
mid-roar, or movie stars tipping their chins.

Their bare ankles in the grass didn't itch.
Through open windows the clatter of dishes

quieted, our mothers' calls stretched
so I could walk between the sounds.

Martial Arts

At the start of every lesson the teacher
asks, *What's your best defense*

in a dark alley? Upstairs our son swings
his legs, kicking neatly like a clock

at the quarter hour, kick
kick punch into the teacher's palms

while we wait in the bar below, knees
touching, watching the news with the sound

off. Someone is wailing but the sound
has left her body. *Don't go down*

the dark alley. The kids stomp
and behind the bar the bottles

chime, a tremble
that ripples back

to the center of itself. Sirens pulse
across the woman's face, the yellow tape

a border keeping
what no one wants to know.

My right knee against your left a small
pressure we've built our house around.

Everything I'm afraid of,
I'm about to name.

Training Exercise

Bluff over the river, burr
oak, unmarked

    burial mound

covered
by a picnic blanket

a girl swinging

    and smoke

curling from a side door
of the old museum

   /

This is only   a drill   only

   one of a swarm

    a charm

   /

In Chagall's *Psalm*
a person etched in a tree

   a person

    in
    the sky

a child's version of a sun

/

Against fear

the sky

its feathers its heralds

/

Straw-colored light:

I've got a gun
          and my dog

a police officer
shouts
              come out—

/

Is there no way
        out of the

          mind?

/

Under the tree
a paper plate

          abandoned

              moon

/

Hidden so long

in another realm
someone
    in the dark museum

believes

    the dog
      lunges

Last Seen

When I was a girl a man in an elevator told me
monkeys pull the cables that move us
floor to floor. He didn't know

I was connected to my body by a string.
Every night my balloon tangled
in the low forest of sleep

while a bear roared, pushing the wind
out of his way, one claw snagging my shoulder.
A cave in front of me. To lose the bear
I disappeared into a world so dark

it held only blind things, and the sound

of a hill accumulating nearby.

Translation

Down from the ladder of sleep
my son comes, taller than the night before

and I a fraction smaller,
allowed a one-armed hug.

Next door an earthmover
is chewing up the scenery,

its vibration in the cages
of my eyes—yet the animals aren't rattled.

The knots of his knees disguised
in new muscle, he comes down from his loft

in solid form and says,
Do you know trees are 90% air?

As if I haven't spent years standing here,
holding my breath.

My Son at Eleven

Nothing in the grass but a slope,
            nothing on the roof

      but rain. The secret of his growth
is just one day: bang

      the yellow lions
            burnishing the field.

II.

I was told

my brother was born with the heart of a bird.
Three chambers not like the rest of us and to live
he must be very strong. *Poor heart, dear heart—*

In their black coats and hats each bird could be
any one, standing in the grass beside a hole.
My brother not like the rest

     red slip/
          feather stitch/
               an opening/

On This Day in History

September 21, 1983

Crucial wreckage is recovered in the Sea of Japan while

closer to home an unheard-of summer freeze—
eight degrees at sunrise—means failure to potato crops

    Futures drift lower

and area searchers find the body of the paperboy

missing since Sunday

         The neighbor lady makes us pancakes
         a little sugar dusted over them

    We are still preserving the scene

        it's Wednesday
        a school day   I'm trying   to get ready

In Beirut, one shell strikes a garden gate and another hits
a swimming pool

    There has been substantial damage

        when my brother
          in a hospital room

     begins hemorrhaging

       the phone rings   the neighbor turns

     her back to me

Time

widens

to a dial tone

Slide

September 21, 1983

A bright day and a silence
that won't advance.

I'm thinking of my mother
and the window she looked into,

not a window really but a square of light
reflected from behind us.

She kept her back to me—
She had a basket braced

against her hip with laundry
to be folded, a length of sheet

or a sleeve dangling.
The basket: a task to hold.

The railing under my hand,
my voice rising,

up the stairs I trailed her,
her shoulders, into the empty frame

of sunlight on the wall.
Since I couldn't see her face

I aimed my question there. That light—
as if we were coming from below

deck on a boat. I felt the whole thing
tilt just before she turned.

Overlay

Like a forest my brother's
body spread its rings.
Atresia: an absence of passage,
a blocked path. Each year
another wreath.
His heart could not keep up.

/

He died of natural causes.
Well-rehearsed
shell
I taught myself to say.

/

Another trail of hidden facts—
In the fall of 1983 and into that
winter there was a manhunt in
Bellevue, Nebraska, for the killer
of 13-year-old Danny Joe Eberle
and another boy, Christopher
Walden.

/

Amnesia: a gap in the story
resulting from shock.
We moved away. I lost
a backyard fort plus
the coffee can with my treasures
—leaf in shale, geode, bones
of field mice kindling.

/

Lost years.
Until my memory handed me
a note about the boys
who'd disappeared.

/

Eberle was found on the day my
brother died. Their obituaries
two adjacent doors, their bodies
alongside each other in the town
cemetery.

/

Part of the heart's anatomy
is the auricle,
little ear.

/

(What's natural?—
not a child's
death.)

/

My memory said, *you dropped this.*
        My son had just turned 10.

/

The path furred, passage blocked.
How had the echo followed me?—

        I'd buried it.

Inside the story of my brother

is the story of the boy
buried next to him.
Inside the boy

a bicycle he kept shined
and a paper route. The route
a Sunday morning,

streetlights snapping off
and the sound of rubber bands plucked
over the folded news. Inside a week

his bicycle against a cyclone
fence, wind-torn papers
wavy with sun and weather.

Inside that abandonment
an exchange, a man rolling down his window,
the boy, barefoot, resting

his bike between his knees.
In this sleepy bedroom town reporters,
circle of searchers, a red pin

on the map: They found the denim shirt
he wore, rope around his wrists.
It's hard to believe in endings

when there's another and
another. Inside the house his parents
were shielded from callers.

Parents calling us inside,
counting our steps from school.
The relentless turning of the clock.

Fear carved an icy well
inside them. Some of them fell.
Some of them could not get out.

Frieze

1.

That winter my mother learning to knit chose yarn the color
of a tooth & stitched her way across the empty field
salt & stalk into the wood where she grew tired
& lay down the long trail tangled around her
my grandmother following took them up
the needles the skein the wilderness
its holes & from them made
a blanket I still have—

2.

Set to ripen on the counter, one pear
never ripens. Winter sun, windowed—

light moves over it and it remains.
This stillness: my father

knuckled over,
hiding his face, his grief.

3.

The door isn't safe
        the window isn't safe
            hide   here

            in this corner here
        with your books
under the cut paper

flowers *Shh* pretend
      you are little seeds
            planted in the garden

            arms and legs curled
      not moving not yet
wait for spring

watch me   wait
      for my signal for
            the cold cloud to pass

Ghosts

beneath a cloud

                                        a cloud shape on the ground

September leaves

                                        trembling

the sound of birds

                                        before the sound of birds
                                        opens   the sky

a small-mouthed gust

                                        standing in for a curtain

The Returned

They've come through the rain
with leaves stuck to their shoes,
hungry, popping cabinets open

and shaking the cereal boxes.
They eat the last of everything.

They don't wonder
if the fish at the bottom of its blue
pebbled bowl is asleep

or dead,
nothing is dead.

Like the insides of teacups
they gleam. Never drowned
or hunted, they have no wounds

on their bodies. They are
where they left off—

So how can we explain our constant longing
for touch, following

and kneeling at doors
closed to us? Wanting to know
what can't be told:

Faces pressed to keyholes,
each room a diorama,

the dressers, combs and the
little shells.

III.

Coming Back

With keys in hand I stood
about to go in
but listening.

The sun lowering,
the tree
projected its blue

needles on my blue front door
and the porch needed
a sweep.

Some wind
lifted.
Everything

was as it seemed and also
in disguise, like
the bird

I'd never heard before saying
what while I thought.
The bent pine

working the lock.
Nearby, unseen:
    What. —

Just that, for a very long time.

Basement

The door needed a shoulder
to shove it open.
Inside:

two parakeets,
a washing machine
that rocked on the damp cement

and a rabbit's cage—the rabbit
sent away because

we didn't love it enough,
my father said.

Oh there was light
graveled
in the window well,

and a string dangled
for a bulb
just out of reach.

Shadow,
  shadow

The soul's oldest room.

Two tiny swings—
one green bird, one blue.

Because I was afraid
they'd escape,
they never flew.

Investigation

Something moved in the grass—wind-roused
feathers—and with them fur
for a doll,

a dried-out cape. The soft pelt
I shouldn't touch, my hand reaching to pet it

unbidden

    unbidden:

The boy's clothes folded neatly
    next to him

        in the snow (red vest)

        in the grove
            of wild plums

At a Distance from Myself I Record the Scene

The teachers are ragged, they think
the afternoon will go on

forever, the rain beginning
to freeze as they huddle

in front of the school in their shirtsleeves
and light sweaters, unprepared

for the headline, *ANOTHER BOY
FOUND*, parents called, every pair

of eyes on watch, every pair
of hands to shepherd younger ones

in their quilted jackets first,
swinging their lunch boxes, then

those without hats, collars turned up,
joking to the light-haired boys,

the look-alikes, *you're next*, shoving,
the older girls scrubbing

their lipstick before
their mothers get a look, and with

sharp whistles to the curb, *not yet,
all right*, the mustached principal

orchestrates, waves the buses in line,
calm down, remain calm,

the doors open, *safely home now*,
he swings his arm

ushering us.

Childhood

huddles, tying its secrets
with the drawstring of its sweatshirt, face half-

hidden. It appears not to hear or maybe
      the distance between you

makes it easier to pretend.
Aren't you cold?   No one

wears a coat.
The air breaks in stiff little clouds
around us. Louise rims her eyes with kohl.

     There was a man in a car.   There is

a man in a tan car with his window rolled down.

     Looking for a boy.

In the labyrinth, keep one hand on the wall.
     Keep one hand on the

     wheel, turning:

Louise teaches me to light a match into the wind-
break of my palm.
The sky is vacant, the bus late.

     The make of the car is lost. Maybe
it wasn't even there

for you to see. Was there a man
at the corner in his car with the window down

     or not?

Site of Disappearance

The wind is a cop with a deadline.
It has one story and you're in the way.

Rattling, it sharpens itself between the door
and jamb. It can stay all night, cool

shiver, scissors near your ear—
your hair falls. The wind repeats its line of questioning

gently now. Look at its softened
rock face. When the world was large you thought

each thing had its god,
god of the redgrass/ god of the river/ god of the eye

but there is less
and less you can remember,

fingerprints erased from the salt dish,
birch trees making scraps of themselves. . . .

Try crawling.
Try reason.

The wind has your name, your
nape in its mouth, and means it.

Biology Lab

First he led us to inspect them,
mice in aquariums lined
with cedar shavings.
As if it were a magic trick
we nodded, and like an audience
we held our breath
when he dropped cotton balls into the tanks
and sealed them. As they died
he put the mice in our hands so we could feel
their heartbeats ease away.
Now you will secure them to the pans,
and we lay them on their backs
and spread their limbs.
We weren't thinking about
the nature of cruelty, though the mice were still
warm. Some of them
twitched as we pinned them.
The light drained from my partner's face.
I wanted to go home. It was dark
and getting late.
Now the first incision down,
then laterally
like an I. You're making a door to go in.
My partner stepped back. The room
was too warm. I picked up the blade and cut,
neck to abdomen.

My Father Wasn't a Hunter

The only time he tried, his brow split open
when the scope kicked back.
Pheasants safe in their grassy hills,
rye in his glass, ice, the shake
of his laugh, recalling.
Recoil the thing that got him.
My father planted a tree between the graves
of my brother and the murdered boy.
Recall. The hunt
for the killer ended on television.
A young man shackled, turning his head away.
Snow on his shoulders.
The sheriff held his elbow,
almost gentle.
The brute syllables of evidence: knife, rope, prints, blood.
Recoil means to shrink from. Recoil means
spring back.
My father furious, talking to the room—
They should take the bastard out and shoot him.

Time Capsule

After the murders, children
in the town dreamed of houses

melting into the sky.
Wind on the down of our necks,
fear riddled its hive inside us.

But as we grew
our memories dwindled

like bicycles now too small to ride.
The graves
lay buried beneath the trees'

shadows. Parents split
and moved away. One sister
survived. She witnessed the dark ceiling
of every midnight

fall into her thoughts.
Reminders kept surfacing: a red bike
hooked to a chain link fence,

a note folded in a pocket
and put through the wash
until she couldn't read it, until

it was grit between her fingers.
You will only be a ghost

sliding through the trees.
This crumbling. Once upon a time
I sank my foot into the shoulder
of a shovel.

IV.

Archive

You can't translate something
that was never in a language
in the first place.
              —Chase Twichell

I took my son
              to kindergarten

I walked him
              to school

I let him walk while I watched   from the window

                              and in that quiet chewed

                                             a nest

My questions as yet

without residence

Marking me:

My body
covered in hives

Brought to light

Whatever begins, begins with

   demand—

In order to rest

   must first be

         examined—

Thousands of miles
in an easterly

direction

A train and I

kept   time

-

Between the radio's silences

rain connected
the side of one state

to

another

Because we are a river town

it is natural to start at the river

Mouth of my childhood

I walked through

The meadow

The cemetery

A tree farm

A middle school hall at the bell

    (pushed by/ sidelined/

        my nickname
           was *Mouse*)

Overheard: A drill

Make yourself as small as possible
                        Protect your neck and throat

And: Someone
counting
down

Boy in a hospital bed

Boy in a freckled field

I went

Because I have

a son at home,

the day's collection
in his pockets:

acorn,   pink eraser,

leaf crumb

In the sparrow's white eye-ring

An eye-ring
Of frost

In the frost-
Starred brush,

The bruise—

                    Where the field assumed
                    A shape

                    The searchers found
                    Their answer

Impressions [of   ]

Human [marks   ]

Whatever begins [

```
bo  y    body
bo  y    body
bo  y    body
bo  y    body
bo  y    body
bo  y    body
body     body
body     bo  y
body     bo  y
body     bo  y
body     bo  y
```

                                              ] begins with

[   ] buried

     by proximity

          time of death

               coloring/ weight/ height/ age

        coincidence

in the plot
     next to

                 my brother

        [to rest]

     [

           examine   ]

I Tell My Son a Story

A man swung an ax
　　　to clear his view. More
　　　　　meadow for the deer,
　　　a mountain parting
the curtains. But now
　　　he noticed strange
　　　　　noises, as if the house
　　　unsettled itself:
coffee cups chimed
　　　in the kitchen where
　　　　　nobody was, and
　　　the rain registered
differently—*plink plink*—
　　　a tiny piano
　　　　　on his shoulder. Soon
　　　every step felt un-
even, his boots
　　　sinking into mud.
　　　　　The deer ran from him
as from a wolf. Looking
at the woodpile he
　　　began to see the trees
　　　　　not as logs he split
　　　but as spirits, each
with a soundtrack
　　　for his ears. The ghost
　　　　　of the ash intoned *life,*
death, life, death, over
and over until
　　　the words became blows.
　　　　　Ring patterns appeared
　　　on the walls, painted
in black ink, and finally,
　　　finally the man ran—

though who can escape
a world peeled away?
When there is nothing
left but to listen.
The beech tree distills
its light into the dark
eyes of the monster.

His Sentence

On Death Row
in the last interview
he said:

> All of the doors
> are being closed
> behind me.

Grief Sequence

i.

    Running ahead in the park,
he turns to my voice—

ii.

    the days like
little pills,
      numbering

            numb
        mouth
          truth dissolved

iii.

Handful of leaves
      handful of fire
            Black can kicked over

iv.

If I make a hole in the fabric,
so as not to look directly.

    If I remove the vowels
from my name, forgoing
any softness—

v.

    a rash
refuses
    to heal

vi.

I   his mother

        I   sister

vii.

     or bystander,
cradling
     my
        arms.

viii.

If I begin to talk to god again,

ix.

        I'd blacked out every memory.

I only meant to make a little hole—

x.

Mothers
forgive me for opening
        these wounds.

V.

Tender

The chin upturned to miss the zipper.

A kiss. *Be kind* I say before I send him out,
even a door suffers a knock.

Bitten nails their beds.

Those lavender eyelids of late winter
flowers and

the heart at night kicking off its covers,

each of us unwound back to the smallest
doll inside ourselves.

My mouth around his infant foot.

Suite Ending with
the Middle School Symphony Orchestra

Once: my fevered
six-month son
rasping on my chest.
All night
upright, his kicking-
horse heart and the mare
of me, rocking,
rocking.

/

Some days
doldrums,
his toy sailboat
centered
in the reflecting pool
needing a little song
to push it.

/

The last time I saw his unclothed body
I don't remember, not knowing it would be the last time.

/

Phantom infant on my hip—
does he carry
the sway of me?
Spoon to his mouth,
his hand grabbing handfuls of my hair.

/

The heart in its stall
stammers,
stamping the edges
for old cues.

/

Folded on my lap,
his coat;

stage lit,
he coaxes
from his bass
its lowest notes—

Only Child

six pairs
of his cast
off shoes

crowd the
doorway
as if

I had
six sons
to greet me

Surrender

Door softly knocking then
    still, greensick sky

    flash light
crawl space
      radio

   /

     Kingdom hushed
   before the

    roaring

   /

A tornado has tiny fingers,
arranges
     its wreckage
   precisely:

pink cotton filling
   a stripped tree,
     teased
       into a beehive

   /

   Oh candied light
    of morning—

To what do we owe?
Let us bow
   and drink at the altar

of Table Still Standing/
    Three Glasses of Water
    Untouched

/

    To whom the prayer
of one who

    survived,
        animals in arms?

        A door
set gently down

        upon them
then the storm

    swiveled on

Filament

Trestle trestle coupling hook his lullaby at two:
Every day I drove to the crossing and raised him waving,
engine—coal cars—heart-thump—thrill—

Long walks to the park
examining   each   daffodil.

And the traveling circus we saw one March,
the animals muddy, straw
stuck to the dragging hems of the child acrobats.

Horse—horse—mirror—sleigh   again and again
            the zoo.

We spoke Pirate at his birthday party, followed
maps I drew to treasure.

Allosaurus Spinosaurus hammer—chisel—claw—

Roman gladiator, sword and shield.

Mummy-wrapped in toilet paper, a pharaoh
on our couch.

            Now ask him, who restored me
                        to wonder:

            Remember?—

                        His long hair flicks
                                    across his eyes.

If the world is always beginning

inside the great body / lamp shine and sway / pintucked / the
heat pleated quilted / newspaper a whisper / folding / back
onto itself /

I not yet / myself— /

bundled / mittened and sent / this way / fox fur rabbit skin /
new flute winter / sun awake / awake / frost burning off /
who is / the white plume / rising / from these needles /

Spell

My parents were young when

     my brother   stopped time

       *

      still in that house

in Green Meadows

     where lawns unrolled
        from the back of a truck

         and saplings
           anchored

new mothers   new fathers

    *

     I can

        go to them
           now

               light

up the stairs
     to their room

          *

       lean to them
          check

Time to wake

cheek to brows

*

eyes

       fevered and shining

In the Stories We Are All Transformed

Out of the forest and down to Main,
a bear wanders headlong
in the fog, past small houses

wearing the blue of their windows.
The bear can't see and is cold

until mother and daughter let their yarn run
onto the floorboards
and answer the door. Ice clings to his fur

so they bring him to the fire.
His great paws have trouble managing
the china cup of broth, and his voice

slides, sometimes honey, sometimes gravel.
His words are not the words of a bear
yet they aren't afraid,

his wet fur separating into spears
in the firelight. In real life he's a prince buried

inside a bear. When the spell comes apart
with a zipper, he steps out wearing his crown.

And the beautiful bear suit like snowmelt,

its astonished jaws

catching softly at his shined shoes?

I pick it up. I put it on.

Notes

The quoted lines by Jenny George that begin this book are from her poem "Mnemonic." "Training Exercise" quotes a line from Sylvia Plath's "Apprehensions": "Is there no way out of the mind?" The phrase "each bird/ could be any one" in "I was told" is from Stanley Plumly's poem "Cedar Waxwing on Scarlet Firethorn."

"Time Capsule": Immense gratitude to Paco and Jaden, fourth grade students in 2016 at Whittier Elementary School in Seattle, for lines I paraphrased that led me to this poem: ". . . houses/ melting into the sky"; "You will only be a ghost/ sliding through the trees."

The epigraph for "Archive" is from Chase Twichell's poem "Downstairs in Dreams." "Archive" references a quote by then Bellevue Police Chief Warren Robinson, discussing the area to be searched for missing newspaper boy Eberle: "Bellevue is a river community"; it is "natural that we want to start at the river." *Omaha World-Herald*, Sunrise Edition, Wednesday, September 21, 1983. "On This Day in History" and "Inside the story of my brother" also quote lines from the *Herald*.

"I Tell My Son a Story" is in response to music by Bartholomaus Traubeck, composed by "playing" a tree's year rings on a special turntable he invented.

"His Sentence": John Joubert was arrested after threatening a teacher at a preschool. He was convicted of murdering Danny Joe Eberle, 13, Christopher Walden, 12, both of Nebraska; and Richard Stetson, 11, of Maine. He was given the death penalty and died in the electric chair in 1996. The quote in this poem is taken from his last interview, on June 24, 1996, with television journalist Carol Kloss of KETV in Omaha, Nebraska.

Acknowledgments

My thanks to the editors of the publications in which these poems, often in earlier versions or with different titles, first appeared:

"In the Stories We Are All Transformed" and "Site of Disappearance," *Cimarron Review*

"Biology Lab" and "Inside the story of my brother," *Crab Creek Review*

"Last Seen" and "On This Day in History," *Electric Literature*

"I Tell My Son a Story," *Evergreen: Grim Tales & Verses from the Gloomy Northwest* (Scablands Books, 2021)

A few lines from "The Returned" were printed by Expedition Press as a broadside in "Broken Broadsides," a series created by Myrna Keliher

"The Returned" and "Training Exercise," *FIELD*

"Childhood," *Jack Straw Writers Anthology*

"Suite Ending with the Middle School Symphony Orchestra," *New Ohio Review*

"Martial Arts" and "Coming Back," *On The Seawall*

"Archive," "At a Distance from Myself I Record the Scene," "Biography," "Frieze," "I was told," "Investigation," "My Father Wasn't a Hunter," and "Swing the Statue," *Radar Poetry*

"Time Capsule," *Seattle Review of Books*

For the time and support they gave me, I'm grateful to the Anderson Center, Ucross, and Jentel Foundations. Thanks especially to Kimmel Harding Nelson Center for the Arts—located in Nebraska City, NE, the residency allowed me to reconnect to the landscape of my childhood and gave me proximity to the archives at the Omaha Public Library.

Thank you to Kevin Craft and the Jack Straw Writer's Program where this project took root, and to the 2015 fellowship cohort.

From the very beginning, Megan Snyder-Camp asked the questions I needed to answer to bring this book into focus. I'm grateful to her and to Kathleen Flenniken, Keetje Kuipers, Becka McKay, Martha Silano, and Kary Wayson for their close reading, guidance, and companionship when I needed them. Jennifer Preisman walked miles by my side while I talked in circles (thank you, Greenlake).

Ryan Molenkamp's "The Visitor" is a poem in and of itself. Abundant thanks to him for giving his permission to feature it on the front cover.

Thanks to Lisa Ampleman at Acre Books for crucial notes on the manuscript, and to Han VanderHart and Amorak Huey at River River Books for pointing me in the direction of Ornithopter Press. Thank you, Mark Harris, for giving this book a home.

I can't express enough gratitude to the people who took the time to listen to my questions and add their memories of a painful time in service to this project: Sallie Allen, Suzanne Rose, and especially Patricia and Jim Flanagan who bolstered my family. *Site of Disappearance* is for my parents, Lois and Patrick Malone, and my brother Ryan Malone—thank you for your love. My brother Michael Malone is in all ways the heart of this book.

Finally, love and thanks always to Shawn Wong for the compass, and to Peter Wong for the light.

About the Author

Born in New Mexico and raised in Nebraska and Colorado, Erin Malone is the author of two full-length collections: *Site of Disappearance*, finalist for the National Poetry Series, and *Hover*, as well as a chapbook, *What Sound Does It Make*. Recent honors include the Coniston Prize and the Robert Creeley Memorial Prize, and residency support from Kimmel Harding Nelson Center, Anderson Center, Ucross and Jentel Foundations. The recipient of grants and fellowships from Artist Trust, 4Culture, Jack Straw, and the Colorado Council on the Arts, Erin formerly taught in Seattle Arts & Lectures' Writers in the Schools program, served as Editor of *Poetry Northwest*, and now works as a bookseller. She lives on Bainbridge Island in Washington State.

Printed in the USA
CPSIA information can be obtained
at www.ICGtesting.com
JSHW020440100923
48057JS00002B/77